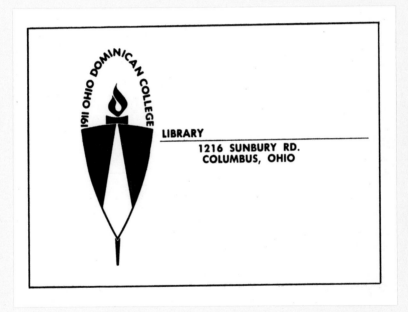

Joseph Sheridan LeFanu

THE IRISH WRITERS SERIES

James F. Carens, General Editor

JOSEPH SHERIDAN LEFANU

Michael H. Begnal

LEWISBURG
BUCKNELL UNIVERSITY PRESS

© 1971 by Associated University Presses, Inc.
Library of Congress Catalogue Card Number: 71-126032

Associated University Presses, Inc.
Cranbury, New Jersey 08512

ISBN: 0-8387-7766-X   (cloth)
ISBN: 0-8387-7735-X   (paper)
Printed in the United States of America

For Cynthia

Contents

Chronology of Sheridan LeFanu

1814: Birth, August 28, at the Royal Hibernian School, Dublin

1826: Family moved to Abington in County Limerick

1831: Tithe Wars and his family's problems with the peasants

1837: Graduated from Trinity College, Dublin

1838: Published first work, "The Ghost and the Bonesetter," in the *Dublin University Magazine*

1839: Called to the Irish Bar, but never practiced

1840: Composed the ballad "Shamus O'Brien"

1841: Became editor and proprietor of *The Warder*

1844: Marriage to Susan Bennett

1845: Publication of first novel, *The Cock and Anchor*

1847: *Torlogh O'Brien;* poor reviews and cessation of novel-writing

1851: Move to Merrion Square, Dublin; *Ghost Stories and Tales of Mystery*

1858: Death of his wife and the beginning of his seclusion

1861: Became editor and proprietor of the *Dublin University Magazine*

1863: Publication of *The House by the Churchyard*, and resumption of novel-writing

1869: Sale of the *Dublin University Magazine*

1873: Publication of his last novel, *Willing to Die*, and his death

Joseph Sheridan LeFanu

1

Beginnings

In a letter to Father Matthew Russell, W. B. Yeats described as follows the current literary situation in Ireland close to the turn of the century:

> It has quite gone out now—our little tide. The writers who make Irish stories sail the sea of common English fiction. It pleases them to hoist Irish colours—and that is well. The Irish manner has gone out of them though. Like common English fiction they want too much to make pleasant tales—and that's not at all well. The old men tried to make one see life plainly but all written down in a kind of fiery shorthand that it might never be forgotten.[1]

Joseph Sheridan LeFanu was one of those old men who, in a good part of his work at least, employed his own kind of fiery shorthand to describe and explain the Irish society in which he lived. Author of fourteen novels, many short stories, poetry, and a verse drama, LeFanu was almost constantly at work throughout his

---

1. Allen Wade, ed., *The Letters of W. B. Yeats* (London: Rupert Hart-Davis, 1954), p. 143.

13

lifetime, recording what he saw around him and chron-
icling Ireland in the latter half of the nineteenth century. Though most of his novels are set specifically in
the English countryside, they become clearer when they
are transferred to an Irish setting. His London is Dublin,
and his English mansions are in actuality the Irish "big
houses" which were fast disappearing from the contemporary scene. Most of LeFanu's work has now fallen
into critical disfavor, and almost all of his novels remain out of print, but those written at the height of
his power, and even his two historical novels, certainly
are deserving of a revival. Strangely enough, his current
reputation, small as it is, rests on his supernatural or
Gothic stories, but even these seem in need of a critical
reevaluation.

Born in 1814 into a family with a strong literary tradition (among his forebears were dramatist Richard
Brinsley Sheridan and the actor Thomas Sheridan),
LeFanu spent the first years of his life at the Royal
Hibernian Military School in Phoenix Park, Dublin,
where his father was the chaplain. His memories of this
time were perhaps to give rise to his examination of
Chapelizod, *The House by the Churchyard,* but in 1826
his family moved to Abington, a country home six miles
outside of Dublin. It was here that the young man was
to come into closest contact with the Irish peasant and
countryman who is often a most sympathetic character
in his work, and here too he first became aware of the
schism which existed in Irish society. The Tithe Wars
destroyed the friendly relations his family had maintained with the peasantry, and brought home to him the

fact that he was of the Anglo-Irish, Protestant ascendancy. The constant tension and opposition between two kinds of Irishmen and two visions of Ireland became a problem and a paradox with which he was to struggle throughout his writing.

As an undergraduate at the then strongly Protestant and Conservative Trinity College in Dublin, LeFanu was completely opposed to the Reform Bill of 1832. At the same time, however, he was sympathetically interested in the struggles of the Catholic majority for freedom and was fascinated with Irish song and folklore. Though preparing himself for the law, LeFanu had begun to write, and in 1838 his first published story, "The Ghost and the Bone-Setter," appeared in the *Dublin University Magazine*. As a boy he had been taken with tales of outlaws and "rapparees," and in 1839, at the suggestion of his brother William, published an Irish version of Lochinvar, "Phaudrig Crohoore," in the same journal:

> But them days are gone by, and he is no more,
> An' the green grass is growin' o'er Phaudrig
>   Crohoore;
> For he couldn't be aisy or quiet at all;
> As he lived a brave boy, he resolved so to
>   fall.
> An' he took a good pike, for Phaudrig was
>   great,
> And he fought, and he died in the year ninety-
>   eight;
> An' the day that Crohoore in the green field
>   was killed,
> A strong boy was stretched, and a strong heart
>   was stilled.

Despite his belief in the Union, LeFanu could not help admiring the courage and dedication of the revolutionary and the patriot, and he was able to see right on both sides of the question.

At this time LeFanu was called to the Irish Bar, but, much to his family's disappointment, he never practiced. William Maubray's struggle in the later novel, *All in the Dark,* may have been his own:

> He wavered in his allegiance to the Bar. He doubted his fitness for it. Had he not money enough for all his wants? Why should he live a town life, and grieve his soul over contingent remainders, and follow after leading cases in objectless pursuit, and lose himself in Bacon's interminable Abridgement, all for nothing?

Instead, he entered wholeheartedly into writing and magazine work, becoming editor and proprietor of *The Warder* and eventually purchasing shares in such journals as the *Protestant Guardian, Statesman, Dublin Evening Packet,* and the *Evening Mail.* In 1840 he wrote the ballad "Shamus O'Brien," which was not to be published until ten years later. The poem was quite popular across Ireland—so much so that Samuel Lover read it often publicly during his tour of America in 1846, appending his own conclusion, in which Shamus escapes to the United States and opens a public house. Soon "Shamus O'Brien" came to be known as Lover's, an honor he was not quite loath to accept, as he wrote to LeFanu's brother: "I would not wish to wear a borrowed feather, I should be glad to give your brother's name as author, should he not object to have it known; but as his writings are often of so different a tone, I would not speak without permission to do so."[2] Like "Phaudrig Crohoore," "Shamus O'Brien" exemplifies LeFanu's affinity for the Nationalist cause in its story of a young man sentenced to death for his part in the Rising of 1798 who escapes the gallows with a last-minute display of heroism. O'Brien is supposedly modeled on a young rebel named Kirby of County Limerick, who was known to LeFanu, and, though the poem is certainly not a masterpiece of English verse, it is easy to see why its fervor was so much appreciated by an Irish audience:

> But if you would ask me, as I think it like,
> If in the rebellion I carried a pike,
> And fought for old Ireland from the first to
> the close,
> And shed the heart's blood of her bitterest
> foes,
> I answer you, "Yes!" and I tell you again,
> Though I stand here to perish, it's my glory
> that then
> In her cause I was willing my veins should
> run dry,
> And that now for her sake I am ready to die.

These two poems, along with the bulk of LeFanu's early short stories, were collected in 1880 by A. P. Graves and published as *The Purcell Papers*. They form a significant body of work for such an aspiring young writer.

Almost all the tales in *The Purcell Papers* were published in the *Dublin University Magazine* between 1838 and 1840. Basically, they are a potpourri, concerned

---

2. Quoted by William LeFanu, *Seventy Years of Irish Life* (New York: Macmillan, 1893), p. 138.

with the many themes which must have been jostling
for recognition in LeFanu's mind. Thus, those such as
"Jim Sulivan's Adventures in the Great Snow" and
"The Ghost and the Bonesetter" are fairly humorous
tales of Irish folklore written in dialect: "Why, thin,
'tis a quare story, an' as thrue as you're sittin' there;
and I'd make bould to say there isn't a boy in the seven
parishes could tell it better nor crickther than myself."
("Ghost") "The Lost Heir of Castle Connor" and "An
Adventure of Hardness Fitzgerald, A Royalist Captain"
are serious vignettes of Irish history which in many
ways foreshadow the historical romances: "There do,
indeed, still exist some fragments of the ancient Catholic families of Ireland; but, alas! what very fragments!
They linger like the remnants of her aboriginal forests,
reft indeed of their strength and greatness, but proud
even in decay" ("Heir"). In "Scraps of Hibernian Bal-
lads," along with "Phaudrig Crohoore," LeFanu issued
a call for serious and intelligent Irish writing and at-
tacked the

> unconscionable literary perverseness of Irishmen them-
> selves, who have preferred the easy task of concocting
> humorous extravaganzas, which caricature with merciless
> exaggeration the pedantry, bombast, and blunders inci-
> dent to the lowest order of Hibernian ballads, to the
> more pleasurable and patriotic duty of collecting together
> the many, many specimens of genuine poetic feeling, which
> have sprung up, like its wild flowers, from the warm
> though neglected soil.

Also, it has been noted that his "A Chapter in the History of a Tyrone Family" may have been an influence on

Charlotte Brontë's *Jane Eyre*. His career was well under way.

In 1814 he was married to Susan Bennett, the daughter of a successful Dublin barrister, and settled down to writing in earnest. LeFanu had greatly admired the Scottish historical romances of Sir Walter Scott, and with *The Cock and Anchor* in 1845, named for a Dublin inn, he began to work with the raw materials of Irish history. The novel is set in Dublin during the first decade of the eighteenth century, the turbulent period following the Battle of the Boyne, and it attempts to capture, on several societal levels, the flavor of the times. The reader is treated to an insight-filled portrait of the Machiavellian Viceroy of Dublin, Lord Wharton, and even to a cameo of the young chaplain, Jonathan Swift. In answer to a question about the Whigs from Joseph Addison,

> "Sir, I am not to be taken by nicknames," rejoined Swift. "I know Godolphin, and I know Lord Wharton. I have long distrusted the government of each. I am no courtier, Mr. Secretary. What I suspect I will not seem to trust—what I hate, I hate entirely, and renounce openly."

Outwardly, the narrative is conventional enough, with its star-crossed lovers, Edmond O'Connor and Mary Ashwoode, kept apart by the evil machinations of Mary's father, Sir Richard, and brother, Henry. After the elder Ashwoode's plan to unite his daughter and the foppish Lord Aspenly fails, it is Henry, beset with debts and blackmailed with a forged letter of credit, who seeks to wed his sister to the nefarious Nicholas Blarden. Needless to say, these attempts are unsuccessful—Mary escapes to her benevolent uncle, Oliver French, with the aid of her faithful maid, Flora Guy—and the evil schemes are defeated. O'Connor, something of a pale hero to begin with, is conveniently wounded in a duel with Mary's brother and spends most of his time in the plot recuperating.

The center of the novel, however, is LeFanu's attempt to get to the heart of the illness which is plaguing the society in which these people move. The rupture of the normal course of things following the wars of William of Orange has resulted in a kind of moral decadence, where nothing exists which will not be sacrificed for material gain. Thus Sir Richard will cheat his daughter out of her estate and sell her to the highest bidder in order to free himself of debt. Henry will offer his sister to a monster in order to save himself from social and financial ruin. Even the kindly Oliver French, potentially a force for good, has removed himself to his country estate to indulge himself with fine foods and wines and to tend his gout. An entire social order is in decay, and its attitude is exemplified in this description of the audience at a cockfight, where all levels of society mix together freely:

> all these gross and glaring contrarieties reconciled and bound together by one hellish sympathy. All sate locked in breathless suspense, every countenance fixed in the hard lines of intense, excited anxiety and vigilance; all leaned forward to gaze upon the combat whose crisis was on the point of being determined. . . . Every aperture in this living pile was occupied by some eager, haggard, or

ruffian face; and, in spite of all the pushing, and crowd-
ing, and bustling, all were silent, as if the powers of voice
and utterance were unknown among them.

Given a situation in such utter chaos, even Nature
has become a malignant force intent on destroying the
unwary. When Sir Richard dies mysteriously of some
sort of stroke, "the wind swept vehemently upon the
windows with a sound as if some great thing had rushed
against them, and was pressing for admission . . . as if
the very prince of the powers of the air himself were
thundering at the casement." Henry, in prison and ultimately hanged, is beset by the phantom of his guilty
conscience which will not leave him in peace: " 'He
comes there—*there*,' he screamed, pointing to the foot
of the bed, 'with all those infernal cloths and fringes
about his face, morning and evening.' " Even the lovers
cannot escape their doom, for Mary wastes away and
dies and O'Connor is later killed at the battle of
Denain in 1712. The only successful figure in the novel
is the insidious Blarden, who dies peacefully in his bed
at an advanced age, having lived to enjoy the fruits of
his underhanded schemes.

Though the novel seems to end in a kind of moral
confusion, with evil rewarded and good destroyed, what
LeFanu is trying to point out is that the great schisms
in Ireland must be healed before all classes of society
destroy themselves. The central figure of the novel is
certainly Henry Ashwoode, whose weakness, vacillation,
and spiritual debility are representative of his class.
Though the house of Ashwoode has fallen into Faulk-
nerian decay, social and moral order could still be at-

tained if the forces of good would only assert themselves. Larry Toole, though something of a stage Irishman, and Flora Guy are trusty servants whose moral fiber remains unweakened. O'Connor's compatriot O'Hanlon, his benefactor Mr. Audley, and even O'Connor himself, are seeking to put society once again upon an even keel. Indeed, LeFanu seems almost to be saying that the Protestant aristocracy has degenerated and must make way for a new and more hardy breed of individual, perhaps represented by the self-made Audley. Political considerations must be put aside for moral ones, and only then can peace and serenity rule in Ireland. *The Cock and Anchor* is social commentary, as well as the costume drama which critics have previously termed it.

LeFanu continued his experiments with the historical novel in 1847 with *The Fortunes of Colonel Torlogh O'Brien: A Tale of the Wars of King James,* and here he poses a solution to the problem which he raised in his first novel. The time is the late seventeenth century, just prior to the Battle of the Boyne, when Ireland was once again torn by strife and James had personally come to Dublin to lead the Royalist forces. S. M. Ellis has said that the tale "can hold its own with the best rivals in the same class of romance,"[3] while conversely Nelson Browne feels it "is almost unreadable now and indeed the novel is amateurish, unbalanced."[4] It is certainly true that LeFanu occasionally becomes a little too melodramatic in the classic nineteenth-century manner: "Oh! for some pitying angel to rescue kindred in-

---

3. *Wilkie Collins, LeFanu, and Others* (London: Constable, 1951), p. 156.
4. *Sheridan LeFanu* (London: Arthur Barker, Ltd., 1951), p. 36.

nocence and beauty. Oh! for some stalworth champion, with righteous heart and iron arm, to hew and crush the cowardly monster into dust." And it is again true, as Browne charges, that scenes of brutality may be a bit overdone, as in the scene of the strappado torture and in this picture of the hideous victim of a fire:

> The head, and one arm and shoulder, as well as one knee, were thrust through the iron stanchions, and all was black and shrunk, the clothes burned entirely away, and the body roasted and shrivelled to a horrible tenuity; the lips dried up and drawn, so that the white teeth grinned and glittered in hideous mockery, and thus the whole form, arrested in the very attitude of frenzied and desperate exertion, showed more like the hideous blackened effigy of some grinning ape, than anything human.

Yet the novel does hold together very well, and its two main plots are unified by a common thematic thread—LeFanu's answer to factionalism.

Balanced against the struggle of the Royalists and Whigs which culminates at the Battle of the Boyne is the attempt of turncoat Miles Garret to wrest the estate of Glindarragh Castle from Sir Hugh Willoughby, a Protestant supporter of William. Ironically enough, Torlogh, from whose family the lands were originally seized, finds himself, as a captain in James's dragoons, in the position of defending Sir Hugh. It is O'Brien who must escort Willoughby, along with his daughter Grace, to Dublin for trial on a trumped-up charge of treason instituted by Garret. After the various plots and counterplots have unfolded, it is Torlogh's personal intervention which saves Sir Hugh, and the brave Irish soldier has won the love of Grace. Torlogh and Hugh, despite their conflicting loyalties, have come to understand and to respect each other, and political and spiritual wounds have been healed. Despite the fact that LeFanu ties this all up perhaps a bit too neatly, what he is demonstrating is that mutual understanding of a common purpose—the rebuilding of Ireland—is the balm which will set all right again.

Throughout the novel, LeFanu, despite his own personal sympathies, has been careful to present both sides in a just and clear light. James himself may be haughty, egotistical, and even a bit licentious, but he is shown as sincerely involved with his cause and with the Irish people. Though Garret and the Duke of Tyrconnell exemplify the evils and opportunism of the Royalist cause, it is Jeremiah Tisdal, a Whig supporter of Sir Hugh, who betrays him at his trial. LeFanu is fair to both Anglo and Gaelic Irish; both have their evil ones. Dick Goslin's English opinion of Ireland: " 'I call it,' he continued with extreme severity, 'a low, dirty, vulgar, 'owling desert,' " is countered by Percy Neville's estimation of the hordes who attack Glindarragh:

> Call them cowards and savages if you will, but as far as I may pronounce from my own poor personal experiences, their flesh wounds smart as much as those of the politest and most valorous people upon earth; and thus much too I will aver, that in this skirmish they have borne themselves as prettily as any men need do.

There is courage on both sides of the lines at the Battles of the Boyne and Aghrim, and symbolically the two camps are to be united in the love of Grace and Torlogh. Here is the hope of the new Ireland—a coming together in love and mutual trust, a turning point away from a contorted past to a vision of a productive and fruitful future.

Unfortunately for LeFanu and for the Irish histori-cal romance, the critical reception of these two works was decidedly cool, and he gave up the writing of novels for quite some time. During the sixteen years following the appearance of *Torlogh*, LeFanu devoted himself to his magazines and published only *Ghost Stories and Tales of Mystery* in 1851. In 1858 his life was drastically changed by the premature death of his wife. Stricken with a grief which was to remain with him throughout his lifetime, LeFanu retired to his home in Merrion Square and, except for the daily trip to his office, vir-tually lived the life of a recluse. Though at home to his family and to friends like the novelist Charles Lever, LeFanu withdrew himself from all other society and came to be known as the "Invisible Prince." Popu-lar legend had it that he could occasionally be seen at night culling the Dublin bookstalls for works on spirit-ualism and the supernatural (it is supposedly at this time that he became involved with the writings of Swedenborg), but for all intents and purposes he was lost to the outside world. The glorification of solitude of Ethel Ware in LeFanu's last novel, *Willing to Die*, might well explain his feelings:

> With the flight of my years, and the slow approach of the hour when dust will return to dust, the love of soli-tude steals on me, and no regrets for the days I have lost, as my friends insist, and no yearnings for a return to an insincere and tawdry world, have ever troubled me. . . . I care for no other. I can love no other; and were I to

live and keep my youth through eternity, I think I never could be interested or won again. Solitude has become dear to me, because he is in it.

It was at this time that LeFanu returned to serious writing, perhaps as a substitute for a life that had been, and it was here that he produced the most valuable and significant portion of his work.

2

LeFanu and the Gothic Tradition

Sheridan LeFanu has been praised for many years as a creator of suspense and of the supernatural, and it is true that a good part of his work is squarely in the nineteenth-century Gothic tradition. In his short stories, especially, he makes great use of the miraculous and the spine-tingling, and Horace Walpole, Charles Maturin, and Edgan Allan Poe are obviously among his literary ancestors. It seems impossible to point to any specific influences, but the Gothic was certainly in the air of the times, witness Dickens and Scott. Like the authors of *Wuthering Heights* and *Jane Eyre*, LeFanu updates the medieval setting of *The Castle of Otranto* and other eighteenth-century Gothic works in an attempt at immediacy and verisimilitude. Walpole's assertion in the first preface to *Otranto* fits LeFanu as well:

> If this air of the miraculous is excused the reader will find nothing else unworthy of his perusal. Allow the possibility of the facts, and all the actors comport themselves

> as persons would do in their situation. . . . Though the
> machinery is invention, and the names of the actors imagi-
> nary, I cannot but believe that the groundwork of the
> story is founded on truth.

Like Melmoth and Heathcliff, most of the protagonists of the stories are men divided against themselves.
They are creatures of violently shifting moods, unable
to control the extreme forces in their natures. Byronic
in character, they plumb the depths and soar to the
heights, and ultimately they are the cause of their own
destruction. Much in the manner of Poe's, LeFanu's
tales oscillate between the poles of supernatural horror
and suspenseful detection. Though he never becomes
involved with logic and deduction (LeFanu offers no
counterpart to Dupin), "The Murdered Cousin" and
"The Evil Guest," for example, are basically concerned
with the unraveling of mystery. The central difference
with the Irishman, however, is that in his development
he will break out of the usual ghost story mold to deal
with a new dimension, and, as in his novels, to relate
his insights to his own society.

Ghost Stories and Tales of Mystery (1851), now an
extremely difficult volume to find, was LeFanu's first
collection of stories of the shadowy and mysterious,
though he had published many singly in magazines.
Two of the pieces, "The Watcher" and "Schalken the
Painter," are based on horror, while the other two
mentioned above are essentially detective thrillers. Captain James Barton in "The Watcher" is pursued by
strange footsteps on his nightly walks, though no physical form can ever be found on his trail. The footsteps

are followed by threatening letters and finally by the apparition of a fellow shipmate whom Barton had doomed to death early in his naval career. Driven almost insane with terror, Barton finds that even total seclusion behind locked doors can provide no escape, for the face of his persecutor appears at the wicket of his garden gate. Ultimately the evil spirit assumes the form of a menacing owl to beard the seaman in his private chamber, where Barton destroys himself as a final release from his pain. The ghost or phantom here is real—no figment of the Captain's imagination—and LeFanu is pointing no moral with his tale. The spirit world is always with us, and we stand in awe of its power to reach out from beyond the grave to claim its vengeance.

The same sort of mythos is being evoked in "Schalken the Painter," as the artist's beloved Rose is given up to the strange Vanderhausen, actually a damned spirit long dead:

> So far all was well; but the face!—all the flesh of the face was coloured with the bluish leaden hue which is sometimes induced by metallic medicines, administered in excessive quantities: the eyes showed an undue proportion of muddy white, and had a certain indefinable character of insanity; the hue of the lips bearing the usual relation to that of the face, was, consequently, nearly black; and the entire character of the countenance was sensual, malignant, and even satanic.

The bizarre and melodramatic are self-evident here. There is no rational explanation of the events in these narratives, and LeFanu is playing upon the innate human fear of the unknown. He is creating dark scenes of terror, populated with what Peter Penzoldt calls "alarming and pugnacious spectres."[1]

"The Murdered Cousin," an expanded version of "A Passage in the Secret History of an Irish Countess," and the basis of *Uncle Silas,* abounds with horror and suspense, yet all the action in the plot is explainable as the machinations of the evil uncle. The young heroine escapes almost by accident, and her cousin is murdered in her place. LeFanu at this time is not much concerned with the exploration of a consciousness, as he will be later in his novel, and the point is purely entertainment. "The Evil Guest," probably the most accomplished story in the volume, is even more heavily shrouded in mystery. Sir Wynston Berkley is murdered in the home of Richard Marston, and, though a servant confesses to the crime, there is something not quite right about the explanation. Marston becomes moody and withdrawn, shuns society, and finally evicts his wife and daughter for the company of the French governess Mademoiselle de Barras. He has visions of Sir Wynston, and even a temporary self-committal to a mental institution is no help:

> Doctor Parkes, whose bedroom was next to that occupied by Marston, was awakened in the dead of night by a howling, more like that of a beast than a human voice, and which gradually swelled into an absolute yell; then came some horrid laughter and entreaties, thick and frantic; then again the same unearthly howl.

The answer revealed after Marston's suicide is that he

---

1. *The Supernatural in Fiction* (New York: Humanities Press, 1965), p. 84.

With descriptions such as that above, LeFanu can be assured of the reader's attention, and the thrust of the theme attains an even greater power. With Conan Doyle, for example, and even with Wilkie Collins to a certain degree, a distance is maintained between the reader and the event, for everything is related in a very calm and cool manner. We view crime and sin in a detached, deductive way, as a puzzle which Sherlock Holmes may solve as an intellectual exercise but not as something which affects him or us very much. It is this very detachment which LeFanu is trying to avoid in his work. Indeed, Doyle's most gripping tale, "The Hound of the Baskervilles," is successful because of the Gothic descriptions of moors and monsters, rather than because of Watson's bumbling or Holmes's ratiocination. There is an aura of the inhuman about Holmes which it is sometimes hard for the reader to overcome. In LeFanu's work the horror is always drawn up close, and life forces itself upon us. There is an enigma in "The Evil Guest," as there is in "The Murdered Cousin," but the emotions of the characters in the stories never allow the reader to abstract himself from the immediate circumstances.

Then too, the forces of evil which confront us are implicit and inherent in ordinary people who are quite like ourselves—not Asiatic fanatics á la Fu Manchu or evil Teutonic scientists and madmen who threaten the existence of the universe. They are sailors, artists, adolescent girls who reflect LeFanu's conviction that evil does not spring from some murky shadowland, but exists right here among us. As was mentioned earlier,

almost all of the stories are developed in a fairly contemporary setting and take place either in Ireland or
England. No one seems to be safe from the touch of the
terrible, and there seems no way in which one might
protect himself. The technique of narrating most of the
tales in the first person heightens the tension even more.
Here lies LeFanu's skill, and here too is the basic moti-
vation for his judicious demonstration of the ghostly
and the monstrous.

As his work develops, he begins more and more to
take us inside his characters, to take a psychological interest in what is happening within the minds of those
who are terrorized and victimized by forces which they
cannot control. Evil may be dramatically described from
the outside, but its delineation can be even more strik-
ing when the artist works from the inside out. Thus as
his writing continued, especially in the short story, Le-
Fanu came to consider not only the origins of evil but
also its effect on the individual human consciousness.
Here is his most decisive departure from a tradition
which had been content with descriptions of action and
outer forms to achieve its objects. The culmination of
this development, as we shall see, is *In A Glass Darkly,*
and certainly LeFanu is, in these stories, no longer at all
involved with the Gothic for its own sake. The center of
his investigations is always the human psyche, and only
from here may significant or valuable statements be
made about the human condition. The conscious and
the subconscious are inextricably locked together, and
only from a description of these separate entities and

an understanding of their interaction can a total vision be accomplished.

The supernatural with which LeFanu is concerned is a universal as well as a particular phenomenon, transcending individual time and place, so that we find in his work little use of the banshee, leprechaun, or other manifestation of Irish folklore. (The vampire of "Carmilla" and "The White Cat of Drumgunniol" are notable exceptions.) His phantoms are essentially unnameable, mainly because each tormented inmate of LeFanu's fiction creates his persecutor out of himself. In the latter part of his career, actually, he seems to relinquish any hearty belief in a spirit world that exists outside the human community, and comes to believe that the individual or the society is responsible for the demon or the monster. No longer does this society or the "common good" contain the answer or solution which can assuage the misery of the individual, so that paradoxically and perversely one becomes one's own torturer. Unfulfilled desires, incomplete aspirations, all contribute to the moral and spiritual decay of the man who once could trust and believe in his God and his country. It is only a step from here to the insights which Freud and Jung were to categorize and expand in succeeding generations, and it is but the same step to the Dubliners whom James Joyce was to paint with so much love and so much hate.

Thus Sheridan LeFanu, in the best of his stories, expects that what he has written will operate on two levels at the same time. The immediacy of the description is meant to bring home the close relationship or kinship between reader and character, while the reader must also view what he is experiencing as something of a psychological case study. When these two facets of his art are working well together, we have LeFanu at his best, pleasing and instructing, as Sidney would say, at one and the same time. His dealings with the supernatural are not the dilettantish dabblings of a Walpole, for always we are brought back to ourselves and to our own time. To LeFanu, the problem of the writer is a serious one, and there is no room for the indulging of one's own foibles and fantasies. As the narrator avers at the conclusion of "The Fortunes of Sir Robert Ardagh," published in the *Dublin University Magazine* in 1838, "The events which I have recorded are not imaginary. They are FACTS."

LeFanu published many tales of this kind throughout his career, but his highest achievement was *In a Glass Darkly,* which appeared near the end of his life in 1872. Framed by the secretary-narrator's arranging of the papers of Dr. Martin Hesselius, a Swedenborgian physician, the tales are carefully arranged as investigations into the ills which plague LeFanu's society. Contemporary life is in a state of rapid disintegration, and the stories discuss, in order, the flaws or misuses of religion, the aristocracy, the law, Romantic love, and sexuality. No longer simply dealing with the thrilling and grotesque, LeFanu is discussing the psychological states of his characters. The horrors are only physical manifestations of the sickness which these people carry within themselves. As E. F. Bleir puts it: "the supernatural is an unconscious element in the mind and it may leap into emergence when the barriers protecting the conscious ego are temporarily broken down, in one case by a drug, in another by a sense of guilt."[4] It is just this guilt which permeates these characters, and each is representative of a stance toward existence which has proved corrupt or no longer workable. Far more terrifying than the suspicion that demons and fiends may perhaps exist is the realization of even more startling terrors within the human soul. It is this grim truth which LeFanu is demonstrating.

Thus, the Reverend Mr. Jennings in "Green Tea" finds himself incapable of performing his duties before his congregation. In the course of composing a book on metaphysics, "the actual religion of educated and thinking paganism," he had fallen into the habit of drinking a pot of green tea nightly, and this, he decides, gave birth to the apparition: "I began now to perceive an outline of something black, and I soon saw with tolerable distinctness the outline of a small black monkey, pushing its face forward in mimicry to meet mine; those were its eyes, and I now dimly saw its teeth grinning at me." Ever near him, the monkey soon destroys his work, sits upon the page when he attempts to preach from the Bible, and finally begins to speak. Its terrible blasphemies drown out his prayers, and, ultimately, despite the intercession of Doctor Hesselius, Jennings cuts his own throat with a razor in order to escape. The Doctor says that this "is the story of the process of a poison, a

4. *Best Ghost Stories of J. S. LeFanu* (New York: Dover Publications, Inc., 1964) , p. viii.

poison which excites the reciprocal action of spirit and nerve, and paralyzes the tissue that separates those cognate functions of the senses, the external and the interior," and the reader can see that the poison is actually a fall from spiritual grace. In his explorations of the religious practices of the ancients, Jennings had come to lose his faith. His intellectual pride had cut him off from God so that he could neither preach nor pray, and the hideous monkey appears from within himself rather than from without. The link or bond between God and man has been broken by man himself, and it is quite possible that LeFanu has Darwin's *The Origin of Species* in mind here. The destruction of God removes a major underpinning from the stability of man's existence, and he can find nothing to replace it.

The transition from the earlier "The Watcher" to "The Familiar" can best be understood in the change of title, for now the evil comes from within Barton and is his intimate rather than the agent of an outside power. As a representative of the aristocracy Barton had pursued his way without thought to the feelings of others. Slowly but surely, the guilt which builds within him over his ruin of a fellow-officer's daughter creates the mental phantom which allows him no peace:

> "I am sure—I *know*," continued Barton, with increasing excitement, "that there is a God—a dreadful God—and that retribution follows guilt, in ways the most mysterious and stupendous—by agencies the most inexplicable and terrific; there is a spiritual system—Great God, how I have been convinced!—a system malignant, and implacable, and omnipotent, under whose persecutions I am, and have

been, suffering the torments of the damned!—yes, sir—
yes—the fires and frenzy of hell!"

Like Jennings, he cannot pray and seems strangely to
have little desire to get well. He has misused his position
and his power, and his death, seemingly from a heart
attack, is a kind of suicide since he almost wishes it on
himself. In much the same way, the title character of
"Mr. Justice Harbottle" has played upon his position
within the law to satisfy his own earthly desires. His
decisions may be purchased for the right sum, and he
does not stick at condemning the husband of his mistress
in order to assure his own domestic tranquility. In a
dream vision near the end of the tale Harbottle is tried
for his crimes by a monstrous vision of himself: "This
Chief-Justice Twofold, who was knocking him about at
every turn with sneer and gibe, and roaring him down
with his tremendous voice, was a dilated effigy of himself; an image of Mr. Justice Harbottle, at least double
his size, and with all his fierce coloring, and his ferocity
of eye and visage, enhanced awfully." Even the blackest
sinner cannot escape the retribution of his conscience,
and Harbottle hangs himself in a kind of atonement for
his sins. Three of the strongest pillars of society: religion,
the aristocracy, and the Law, have become perverted and
debased, and the suicides of their three representatives
point up the hopeless, despairing state in which society
finds itself at this moment. Nelson Browne suspects
that "Dr. Hesselius is, of course, a projection of the
author himself, with his absorption in psychic matters,
and with the strain of Swedenborgian speculation which

characterized his thought in later years,"[5] but neither LeFanu nor Hesselius seems to have the antidote for the patient's ills.

In "The Room in the Dragon Volant" LeFanu turns to the problem of naïve, romantic love in his tale of a young Englishman, Richard Beckett, who is making his tour of the Continent soon after the first overthrow of Napoleon. The young man is taken in by swindlers who wish to divest him of his fortune, and he proves only too willing a victim in his blind love for the beautiful and mysterious Countess de St. Alyre. Though she is married and though he knows nothing about her, he is willing to offer her his wealth in a mad escape to Switzerland: "There was I, ready to brave all dangers, all right and reason, plunge into murder itself, on the first summons, and entangle myself in consequences inextricable and horrible (what cared I?) for a woman of whom I knew nothing, but that she was beautiful and reckless." In his blind idealism, he will throw honor and duty to the winds, and here, says LeFanu, is but another flaw in our society. The substitution of the *beau geste* for responsibility has eroded our moral fiber, though Beckett is to be rescued at the very brink of disaster. Through the effects of the drug *Mortis Imago,* the death of illusion, which the Countess has slipped into his wine, Beckett is incapable of movement but his mental faculties are unimpaired, and he is able to realize what a fool he has been. He is saved from interment alive at the last moment by the French detective Carmaignac, and allowed a second chance. The follies of youth are certainly understandable and excusable, but the passions cannot be allowed to dominate the intellect. To allow them to do so is selfish weakness rather than idealism, and represents but another contributing factor in society's decay.

The concluding story of *In A Glass Darkly* is "Carmilla," and it is for this classic tale of vampirism and Lesbian love that Sheridan LeFanu is most often remembered. Supposedly it provided the inspiration for Bram Stoker's *Dracula,* and it is almost always mentioned in any study of vampire lore. Along with the standard description of monstrosity, LeFanu blends a languor and attraction which make of the situation a strange kind of approach-avoidance. Laura, the victim of the vampire, narrates the events which follow the appearance of the evil Carmilla at the family castle; the growing attachment of the two girls points to something more intimate than mere friendship:

> From these foolish embraces, which were not of very frequent occurrence, I must allow, I used to wish to extricate myself; but my energies seemed to fail me. Her murmured words sounded like a lullaby in my ears, and soothed my resistance into a trance, from which I only seemed to recover myself when she withdrew her arms.
>
> In these mysterious moods I did not like her. I experienced a strange tumultuous excitement that was pleasurable, ever and anon, mingled with a vague sense of fear and disgust. I had no distinct thoughts about her while such scenes lasted, but I was conscious of a love growing into adoration, and also of abhorrence.

Once the vampire is discovered in their midst, the plot moves swiftly to Carmilla's gory and dramatic destruction, but the bulk of the story is a description of the girls' relationship. Certainly LeFanu's purpose here is not to attack the practice of homosexuality, but rather to comment on the self-destruction of a total submission to sexuality. Just as Carmilla will drain the life's blood from her prey, so too will lust destroy the moral and physical lives of its victims. Though Laura's father takes her on a tour of Italy to forget what has happened, the phantom will not be exorcized: "to this hour the image of Carmilla returns to memory with ambiguous alternations . . . and often from a reverie I have started, fancying I heard the light step of Carmilla at the drawing-room door."

Peter Penzoldt asserts that "it is doubtful whether LeFanu ever knew it, or was aware of the true nature of what he was describing [in "Carmilla"],[6] but the total structure of *In a Glass Darkly* would tend to prove him wrong. Behind the window dressing of vampirism LeFanu is presenting a study of aberrant sexuality and fitting it into a more general critique of society. The citizens of this world have given themselves up to corruption and the pleasures of the flesh, and it is this failure, symbolized and pointed up by the appearance of the supernatural, which has given evil a free hand. In his perceptions into individuals, LeFanu has learned that it is human actions which create spirits and fiends, and that it is the soul which must be cleansed. If he sounds like a moralist, this is, on one level, exactly what he wishes to be. He can offer no solutions, as he cannot in the majority of his novels, but he can at least locate

---

6. *The Supernatural in Fiction*, p. 75.

the center of the problem. The shift in intent and technique from *Ghost Stories and Tales of Mystery* to *In a Glass Darkly* is indicative of LeFanu's growth as an artist. In this final collection of stories he has grouped them all around a common motif and made the Gothic or supernatural an integral part of his statement. Here again Walpole's Preface would seem applicable to Le-Fanu, whose concern is not only to titillate, but to educate. Further, in his tight structuring of his materials he demonstrates an artistic control which is a tribute to his talent.

3

LeFanu the Novelist

Emerging from the early years of LeFanu's seclusion
were the four most powerful and consistent novels which
he was to write: *The House by the Churchyard* (1863),
Wylder's Hand and *Uncle Silas* (both published in
book form in 1864), and *Guy Deverell* (1865). Though
different in their intents, they display LeFanu the novelist at the high point of his career in the strengths of
their characterizations and the masterful control of their
plots. They are not merely thrillers or "sensation
novels"; rather, these works are attempts at insights into
both the individual psyche and the spirit at the heart
of his contemporary society. They rely for their strengths
on the exploration of personality, rather than on a horrible or shocking situation. While it no doubt is true
that LeFanu's power ebbs in some of his later work, and
that more and more he relies on the grotesque for his
effect, it is here in these early novels that he may claim
a rightful place beside Dickens and Walter Scott.

In 1861 Sheridan LeFanu had purchased and become
editor of the *Dublin University Magazine,* a position he

was to retain until 1869, and had immersed himself in
the writing of articles and reviews. It was in this journal
in 1861 that the first installment of *The House by the
Churchyard: A Souvenir of Chapelizod* appeared under
the pseudonym of "Charles de Cresseron," an ancestral
family name of LeFanu's. Here, in this examination of
life in a Dublin suburb, the novel treats Irish society on
almost all its levels, from the aristocratic Mervyn's fight
to redeem his family's name to the trials and tribulations of the townspeople and the soldiers of the Royal
Irish Artillery. Though a good part of the novel is concerned with the mysterious Charles Archer and the
search for the murderer of the army doctor Sturk, the
bulk of the narrative traces, from one level of society to
another, the lives and fortunes of the town's many inhabitants. *The House by the Churchyard* has been at-
tacked on the grounds that its plot unfolds too slowly
and that its focus jumps too swiftly and erratically from
character to character, but in fact LeFanu is creating
here a microcosm of a larger society. To V. S. Pritchett,
"his comic subalterns, scheming land agents and quar-
reling doctors, his snoring generals and shrill army
wives, are drawn close up, so close up that it is rather
bewildering until you are used to the jumpy and awk-
ward angles of his camera."[1] The fates of Lily Walsingham, the rector's daughter, and Lieutenant Puddock,
the lisping poet, are just as important and significant,
says the novel, as the unmasking of the villain, Paul
Dangerfield.

---

1. *The Living Novel and Other Appreciations* (New York: Random
House, 1964), p. 127.

The narrator of the chronicle, the simple and loquacious de Cresseron, became interested in the story when, as a boy, he was present in the churchyard of Chapelizod at the discovery of a battered human skull, later revealed to be that of Doctor Sturk. In an agreeable and chatty tone, he goes on to unfold the events which led up to the mysterious bludgeoning of the surgeon, the mistaken allegations against Lord Castlemallard's agent, Charles Nutter, and the momentary recovery of Sturk after the trepanning performed by the disreputable Black Dillon, "possessing the power of a demigod, and the lusts of a swine." Dorothy Sayers says that this scene "in itself would entitle LeFanu to be called a master of mystery and horror."[2] Sturk's dying words reveal Dangerfield to be both his attacker and the evil Charles Archer, and the latter is finally captured after a fierce struggle in his strange home, the "Brass Castle." Dangerfield himself is a study in total villainy, describing himself as "half man, half corpse—a vampire—there is no rest for thee: no sabbath in the days of thy week. Blood, blood—blood—'tis tiresome." When it is found that Archer was responsible for a previous murder which was falsely attributed to Mervyn's father, another problem is solved and the town is left to recover from its shock:

> The wher-wolf had walked the homely streets of their village. The ghoul unrecognized had prowled among the graves of their churchyard. One of their fairest princesses, the lady of Belmont, had been on the point of being sacrificed to a vampire.

2. *The Omnibus of Crime*, ed. Dorothy Sayers (New York: Garden City Publishing Co., 1929) , p. 24.

Despite the fact that Dangerfield is continually described as some kind of horrible monster, it should be noted that neither he nor his unwilling accomplice, the sexton Ezekiel Irons, are in any way connected with the supernatural. Dangerfield may be called "a phantom, with the light of death and the taint of the grave upon him . . . dogged by inexorable shadows through a desolate world, in search of peace," but it is malice and avarice, human flaws, which seem to transform him. Human evil, LeFanu seems to be saying once again, is far more horrible and terrifying than anything from beyond the grave, and it is far more abnormal in the change it can work upon an individual. As a nod to the supernatural, LeFanu does include the history of Mervyn's residence, the "Tiled House," with its ghostly hand which had always threatened the place's inhabitants:

> Mrs. Prosser, quite alone, was sitting in the twilight at the back parlour window, which was open, looking out into the orchard, and plainly saw a hand stealthily placed upon the stone window-sill outside, as if by someone beneath the window, at her right side, attempting to climb up. There was nothing but the hand, which was rather short but handsomely formed, and white and plump, laid on the edge of the window-sill.

Though this has been called "the most terrifying ghost story in the language,"[3] it still cannot be compared in diabolism with the machinations of Dangerfield, and the irrational does not enter into the novel again. Every incident in the narrative is explainable; the point is

---

3. S. M. Ellis, *Wilkie Collins, LeFanu, and Others*, p. 158.

that it is far more shocking to realize that such evil is the product of a human brain.

The strength of *The House by the Churchyard* lies in its characters, LeFanu continually giving each of his creations a few moments before the footlights. As Elizabeth Bowen has noted, "his hero-less plot is kept spinning by a diversity of criss-crossing passions."[4] Our narrator tells us that "the honest prose of everyday life is often ten times more surprising than the unsubstantial fictions of even the best epic poets," and it is this very chattiness and homeliness which James Joyce seized upon in structuring his own tale of Chapelizod, *Finnegans Wake*. If any of the characters might be said to live, one must certainly turn to the beautiful and ill-fated Lily Walsingham and her handsome lover, Captain "Gypsy" Devereux. Just as Devereux cannot overcome his liking for brandy and gambling, so Lily's fragility cannot exist for long amid the harsher realities of life. The scene of her death from consumption is most touching, because LeFanu manages to evade the maudlin and turns our attention instead to the grief of the Captain and the elder Walsingham. In contrast to this unhappy affair is the romance of Mervyn and the statuesque Gertrude Chattesworth, complete with secret meetings and the eventual happy uniting of the pair. Besieged by the suit of Dangerfield and the urgings in his direction from her Aunt Rebecca, Gertrude remains true to her love and gives an almost complete picture of upper-class life in eighteenth-century Ireland.

---

4. Introduction to *The House by the Churchyard* (New York: Stein & Day, 1968), p. x.

On another level are the many humorous and amusing characters who abound in the novel. The bristling Lieutenant Fireworker O'Flaherty just escapes becoming a caricature, but the scene of his duel with Nutter is a fine piece of comic art. Just so, Lieutenant Puddock is often ludicrous in his romantic longing for the unattainable Gertrude and in the pratfalls he takes with his friend Cluffe, yet his sympathy and understanding of the tortured Devereux give an added human dimension to his character. Aunt Rebecca, a stereotyped maiden aunt later united to Puddock, becomes real in her understanding of her unhappy niece, and even the coquettish Magnolia Macnamara comes alive in her verbal sparring with the less well endowed ladies in her circle. In counterpoint to the Dangerfield situation, then, are the lives of many different sorts of people, and the places like Phoenix Park which seem to live in themselves. We are expected to fit these all together, like the pieces in a mosaic, to form a comprehensive view of Chapelizod. *The House by the Churchyard* is perhaps not quite high art, but it is certainly a fine presentation of humanity, with its foibles, fiends, and friendships. The narrator's farewell is indicative: "So I pull my night-cap about my ears, drop the extinguisher on the candle, and wish you all pleasant dreams."

Wylder's Hand, though completely different in theme and technique from his previous work, is probably Sheridan LeFanu's greatest accomplishment. Here he certainly surpasses Wilkie Collins, to whom he has often been compared. Once again the narrator is de Cresseron, but now he is a young man, both having more insight and being more directly involved in the action. With very few minor exceptions the central plot is always in the foreground, and a strong emphasis is placed upon the narrative as well as on character. Mystery and suspense are paramount, and, in Stanley Lake, LeFanu presents a character the equal of Dangerfield in villainy. Rachel Lake, Stanley's sister, adds another dimension and perspective to the book; it soon becomes clear that *Wylder's Hand* will center upon individual psychological portraits rather than on any larger study of society in general.

The plot revolves around Stanley Lake, who has displaced his rival, Mark Wylder, by marrying the stately and capricious Dorcas Brandon and assuming control of her estates. The mystery which puzzles and disturbs everyone is that Wylder has disappeared after a shadowy confrontation with Lake, though letters purporting to be his continue to arrive from various locations on the Continent, breaking his engagement with Dorcas and issuing business directives to his attorney Larkin. Rachel and Stanley share the hidden knowledge which is the key to the mystery, but the reader is held in suspense as the noose slowly tightens. Larkin himself has begun his own investigation:

> This little parcel of letters was, in its evil way, a holy thing. While it lay on the table, the room became the holy of holies in his dark religion; and the lank attorney, with tall bald head, shaded face, and hungry dangerous eyes, a priest or a magician.

Ultimately it is revealed that Lake had murdered Wylder in a brawl and, with his sister's aid, buried the body;

the letters had been forgeries, posted from the Continent by a henchman of Lake. The most gripping moment of the novel incorporates this revelation with the death of Lake. Prosperous now, and engaged in running for a seat in the House of Commons early in the spring, Lake is thrown from his horse and killed when the beast shies from Wylder's pointing hand, which the rains have uncovered:

> It was, indeed, a human hand and arm, disclosed from about the elbow, enveloped in a discoloured coat-sleeve, which fell back from the limb, and the fingers, like it black, were extended in the air. . . . In this livid hand, rising from the earth, there was a character both of menace and appeal; and on the finger, as I afterwards saw at the inquest, glimmered the talismanic legend "Resurgam—I will rise again!"

What makes Lake so interesting as a character is that, despite his glinting yellow eyes, he is not at all the completely diabolical figure that was Dangerfield. In actuality Lake is rather weak, and he is tortured throughout the novel by guilt for what he has done and fear that he will be discovered. One act of villainy leads him into the necessity for another; he is never left able to gloat over his gains. Nelson Browne has praised the characterization of Mark Wylder,[5] but it is in Lake that LeFanu describes the ravages of evil in the human soul. The reader cannot help being a bit sympathetic toward the murderer, for he is not a cardboard figure but a human being in torment, estranged from all of those around him whom he once loved. Confession could re-

---

5. *Sheridan LeFanu*, p. 44.

vitalize his relationship with his wife, Dorcas, and
cement his sister's love, but this is a step to which he
can never bring himself. He is spiritually damned, and
his fall brings his house down around many others as
well as himself.

Another strong point in *Wylder's Hand* is LeFanu's
depiction of women, a talent to become even more ap-
parent in his later novels. Dorcas is a willful girl, pas-
sionately in love with Stanley, yet something in her
emotional makeup will not allow her to make her feelings plain. She cannot communicate with her husband,
and the omnipresent secret, of which she is dimly aware,
damages the close ties she had had with her friend.
Rachel herself is being destroyed by her horrible knowledge (she must refuse the proposal of Lord Chelford),
and all her being is directed toward convincing Stanley
that an admission of what has happened must be made at
least to Dorcas. All three characters move paradoxically
in a situation of love and distrust; only the fatal accident
can resolve the tension. Though Rachel is instrumental
in foiling the insidious Larkin's plan to swindle the Reverend William Wylder, Mark's brother, she can do
nothing to save either her loved ones or herself.

Deep in the fabric of this tale is a sense of impending
tragedy and doom, and no happy ending is offered.
Scarred by their psychological ordeal, Rachel and Dorcas
withdraw themselves from society for a life of travel, and
de Cresseron last sees them by accident in Venice:

> The song ceased. The gondola which bore the musicians
> floated by—a slender hand trailed its fingers in the water.
> Unseen I saw. Rachel and Dorcas, beautiful in the sad

moonlight, passed so near we could have spoken—passed
me like spirits—never more, it may be, to cross my sight
in life.

Gone now is the optimism about the state of things
which LeFanu had felt in his early novels, replaced by
a feeling that life is a dark vale through which a man
must travel alone. Accident and mischance are more the
elements of existence than form and order, and one's
goal must be changed to survival instead of triumph.
Wylder's Hand is a dark vision, but it is a masterfully
constructed one. The praise of fellow-novelist Charles
Lever is its most fitting tribute:

> I cannot wait for the end of the month, and the end of
> your story, to tell you of a very serious blunder you have
> made in it. . . . Your blunder was in not holding back
> your novel some twelve or fifteen years, for you will never
> beat it—equal it you may, but not pass it.[6]

In 1864, once again published initially in the pages
of the *Dublin University Magazine,* came *Uncle Silas:
A Tale of Bartram-Haugh,* considered by many to be
LeFanu's masterpiece. As an indication of its appeal,
it has been dramatized for the stage and fairly recently
even made into a movie. The tale is expanded from a
short story of his called "A Passage in the Secret History
of an Irish Countess," which had been originally published in 1838—a technique of composition which the
novelist was several times to employ. Prefacing the work
is "A Preliminary Word," in which LeFanu explains
the previous publication and seeks to defend himself
against the charge that he is a writer of "sensation

6. Quoted in Ellis, p. 160.

novels." Acknowledging his debt to Sir Walter Scott, he points to scenes of horror in *Ivanhoe, Old Mortality,* and *Kenilworth* that are not artistic blots on their surfaces, and states that his novel observes "the same limitations of incident, and the same moral aims." *Uncle Silas,* he says, is a member of "the legitimate school of tragic English romance." Most significant is LeFanu's claim to moral aims in his work, for this element of his writing has been consistently overlooked. As well as writing a thrilling mystery (Arthur Conan Doyle is said to have used the plot for his *Firm of Girdlestone*), LeFanu is once again examining the manifestation of evil in but another of its palpable forms.

Maud Ruthyn narrates the story in her own words, demonstrating LeFanu's highly developed competence with first-person narration, and actually reveals to the reader as much about herself and her own psychology as she does about those who surround her. She is under the care of her father Austin Ruthyn of Knowl, a Swedenborgian in whom the writer supposedly created a self-portrait, but at the latter's death her guardianship is transferred to her Uncle Silas. All this has been accomplished at the express command of her father, since the imputation of murder, lodged against Silas in the past but never proved, has cast a shadow over the family name. The shadow would be lifted if Silas could demonstrate his good intentions in the guidance of his wealthy niece. Maud accepts Silas in all good faith, and her days are made more interesting by the friendship she forms with her untutored cousin Milly as they explore the premises of the estate of Bartram-Haugh.

Slowly but surely tension builds, accomplished the more convincingly in that we view events entirely through the consciousness of Maud. Though Silas seems friendly enough, his peculiarities are disturbing—he partakes freely of opium and laudanum and at times is almost maniacally religious. Maud is affronted by the crude advances made by Silas's son, Dudley, and shocked by the brutality of the foreman Pegtop Hawkes. In addition Maud is burdened by memories connected with her foreboding former tutor Madame de la Rougierre, and by the nagging suspicion that Dudley strongly resembles a man who took part in an attempted kidnaping of Maud while she was in the company of the Frenchwoman. Strangely enough, even the less attractive figures have their appealing aspects, for Silas is often kindly and Dudley capers like a country buffoon, but it soon becomes clear that Silas expects that Maud and Dudley will marry and that her fortune will become one with that of her uncle. At the unexpected news that Dudley is already married to a tavern wench, Silas displays something more of his true nature:

> I never saw such a countenance—like one of those demon-grotesques we see in the Gothic side-aisles and groinings—a dreadful grimace, monkey-like and insane—and his thin hand caught up his ebony stick, and shook it paralytically in the air.

Milly having been sent away to school in France, the plot is brought completely into the open. Rougierre reappears; Maud is made a prisoner while the conspirators consider how best to accomplish her death—her prison the exact same room in which a murder had taken place years before. By exchanging the drugged wine meant for her with Madame, Maud is able to escape while Dudley mistakenly murders the sleeping Frenchwoman: "there came a scrunching blow; an unnatural shriek, beginning small and swelling for two or three seconds into a yell such as are imagined in haunted houses." From this moment on, however, the solid front of evil shatters into fragments. Dudley is shaken and repulsed at what he has done and escapes immediately to Australia; Silas takes to his room and dies later that night from an overdose of laudanum. Rather than ending on a note of happiness with virtue and goodness preserved, Maud speaks mainly of her sorrows, of the death of her first child after her eventual marriage to Lord Idbury, and of her feeble hope that life will not deal too harshly with her in the future.

Once again LeFanu is dealing ironically with the impending doom which seems to lie at the center of human life. Silas is more closely akin to Stanley Lake than to Paul Dangerfield, for he is driven to his deeds as much by circumstances as he is by any innate lust for evil. In his depiction of the Ruthyns of Bartram-Haugh LeFanu is presenting aristocracy gone to seed, the degeneration of a once noble family to a base and futile people grasping for money and power. Once Silas sees his offspring Dudley for what he really is—a low and insensitive conniver—the senseless murder becomes as much an act of self-destruction for the Ruthyns as an attempt to regain lost position. The actual subject here is Ireland; Elizabeth Bowen was the first to recognize the characteristic "hermetic solitude and the autocracy of the great country house, the demonic power of the family myth, fatalism, feudalism and the 'ascendancy' outlook."[7] Miss Bowen is almost offensively condescending to what she terms a "race of hybrids," but to the novelist they are a serious matter.

Maud Ruthyn is a character to whom the reader is sympathetic, much in the way one is sympathetic to the heroine of a Jane Austen novel, but she lacks the moral assertiveness to stand up to life. Fears and terrors seem to lurk all about her, and she is completely at a loss as to what she might do about them. Her father had withdrawn from the world, much as had Oliver French and LeFanu himself, to study with the Swedenborgian Doctor Brierly, and her cousin Milly has been left to grow up untended like a weed, completely unaware of any culture or of her heritage. Balancing the weakness of these high-born characters is the innate strength of commoners like Madame de la Rougierre[8] and Pegtop Hawkes. Brutal these people may be, but they somehow have the knowledge and ability to deal with life on its own terms, to fight back against their own circumstances. The rude and untutored Meg Hawkes, for example, has the resourcefulness which Maud so badly lacks, and "Beauty" also possesses a strength and vitality which should mark her for survival. The nobility is

---

7. Introduction to *Uncle Silas* (London: Cresset Press, Ltd., 1947), p. 8.

8. S. M. Ellis says that "she had a prototype for some of her physical and mental characteristics in the person of a Swiss governess who had terrorised LeFanu in his early childhood." *Wilkie Collins, LeFanu, and Others*, p. 163.

surrounded and doomed, and, if the comparison is not too much, it appears that the Irish Snopeses will inherit the earth.

Thus *Uncle Silas* does have a moral, and a sociological one at that. Much like Dostoevsky in his technique here, LeFanu has woven into a fairly stock mystery or detective story an evaluation of his culture, successfully pleasing and instructing at one and the same time. Though no more than an outward comparison can be made between the Irishman and the Russian in relation to narrative power, it is important to recognize the fact that LeFanu lives up to the claims he makes in his Preface. In leaving society physically he has not given it up spiritually, and from his seclusion comes the evaluation which most of his peers are unwilling or unable to make. LeFanu may have been able to forgo the pleasure of the company of his fellow countrymen, but it is obvious that he could not suppress his concern for them.

Guy Deverell is the concluding volume of LeFanu's important quartet of novels, and it may be seen as something of a continuation of the theme he had been treating in *Uncle Silas*. The basic confrontation here is between Sir Jekyl Marlowe, usurper of the estate of Marlowe Manor, and Monsieur Varbarriere, otherwise Herbert Strangways, the disguised friend of Sir Jekyl's victim. Present, but seemingly aloof from the conflict, are Guy Deverell, the son of the slain man, and Beatrix Marlowe, the daughter of Sir Jekyl. It is the intention of Varbarriere to destroy Jekyl and to restore the estate to its rightful owner. He is portrayed as a kind of cross between Prospero and an avenging angel:

> Grey, heavily projecting eyebrows, long untrimmed moustache and beard; altogether a head and face which seemed to indicate that combination of strong sense and sensuality which we see in some of the medals of Roman Emperors; a forehead projecting at the brows, and keen dark eyes in shadow, observing all things from under their grizzled penthouse, these points, and a hooked nose, and a certain weight and solemnity of countenance, gave to the large and rather pallid aspect . . . something as we have said, of the character of an old magician.

Given such a forbidding aspect, we should expect that Jekyl would need to be something of a formidable opponent, but in reality he is little more than a fairly interesting rake, past middle age and concerned more with his gout and receding hairline than he is with his enemies. Varbarriere, too, fails to live up to his advance billing. His plan to alert the husband of Lady Jane Lennox, with whom Jekyl is having an affair, so that a duel will be necessitated, nearly fails when the avenger almost has a change of heart. The actual discovery, with General Lennox hiding behind a curtain with a dagger, and Jekyl approaching his love through a secret passage behind the walls, is close to lapsing into bedroom farce, though Jekyl is wounded and finally does die. Guy, after learning something of his guardian's plans, has refused to participate and has left the mansion to dream of Beatrix, with whom he has fallen in love. Thus the revenge is accomplished, but it certainly is not sweet, and one at first feels that something must be lacking.

What is again at issue in this tale is the regeneration of the aristocracy. LeFanu is indicating that retribution and the redressing of wrongs are not at all the right way. The plots here seem senseless, a vestige of a past which neither side can remember very clearly and which can serve no purpose. In one instance Varbarriere seems beginning to like Sir Jekyl, but a misguided sense of justice drives him on. Jekyl himself is harmless and almost blameless, his killing of Guy's father resulting from firing too quickly in a duel; the problem could much better have been resolved by arbitration and reconciliation. The antagonists might well be tottering veterans of the Boyne, refighting their battle on the back lawn, and the thematic implication here appears at first much like that of *Torlogh O'Brien*.

Hope for the future, LeFanu seems to be saying, rests with the young, with the lovers Guy and Beatrix. They are not much concerned with old feuds and would much rather be left alone to deal with the present and the future—a much more realistic point of view. It should be mentioned, however, that there are two flaws to this happy solution—the first being that the lovers are both flat and pallid as characters. It is hard to believe in these two as the rejuvenation of a social class when one cannot really believe in them as people. They move with a kind of ennui through the action and definitely do not display the kind of élan one might expect from a new breed. The second stumbling block resides in LeFanu's own outlook, for the old sense of tragedy and defeat looms behind his pages. The conclusion of the novel

tells us that Guy and Beatrix have been married, but
the final word is left to the grieving Lady Jane:

> "Where is he? How can I reach him, even with the tip
> of my finger, to convey that one drop of water for which
> he moans now and now, and through all futurity." Vain
> your wild entreaties. Can the dumb earth answer, or the
> empty air hear you? As the roar of the wild beast dies in
> solitude, as the foam beats in vain the cold blind preci-
> pice, so everywhere apathy receives your frantic adjuration
> —no sign, no answer.

It is almost as if LeFanu would like us to believe, and
would like to convince himself, that an answer can be
found, but ultimately he cannot keep up the pretense.
Ironically, *Guy Deverell* says on its surface what it con-
tradicts at its core. Swinburne found the novel "too
hasty, too blurred, blottesque," and this may be the
reason. LeFanu had bravely begun to point a way out
of the quandaries indicated in *Wylder's Hand* and *Uncle
Silas,* but the optimism and promise which had bolstered
the historical romances had become depleted. Whether
his final position at the end of these four novels is that
of a realist or a pessimist is something which cannot be
discussed profitably here, but taken together these works
constitute a significant comment on the Irish social and
political scene. What is the position of the Anglo-Irish,
he asks; what can be done to unite their aims with Ireland's and to ward off their steady spiritual demise?
It is no discredit to Sheridan LeFanu that he was not
capable of providing viable answers to questions such
as these; it *is* to his credit that he raised questions ab-
solutely central—the modern experience of his nation.

LeFanu continued to produce a novel yearly, but something seems to be lacking in these novels of his middle period. *All in the Dark* (1866), for example, is little more than the description of a Victorian romance, and the novelist does not really have his heart in his work. William Maubray is not very lifelike in his struggle for the hand of Violet Darkwell, and it is also hard to believe that his Aunt Dinah, or LeFanu himself for that matter, can take the tacked-on spiritualism and table-tapping very seriously. Character here is not explicated at any great depth, and William's sleepwalking and the discovery that he is his own ghost are certainly anticlimactic. The main problem with *All in the Dark* is that the plot never seems quite sure where it is going. The marriage of William and Violet is a foregone conclusion, and the minor obstacles thrown in their way are something neither they nor we ever worry about very much.

The Tenants of Malory (1867) is noteworthy for the reintroduction of Mr. Larkin, the scheming lawyer of *Wylder's Hand,* and for the creation of Mr. Dingwell, a character who may rank with some of the best portraits of Dickens:

> You know how death and sin came into the world, and you know what they are. Sin is doing anything on earth that's pleasant, and death's the penalty of it. Did you ever see anyone dead, my sweet child?—not able to raise a finger or an eyelid? rather a fix, isn't it?—and screwed up in a stenching box to be eaten by worms—all alone, underground? You'll be so, egad, and your friend Jemmie, there, perhaps before me—though I'm an old boy. Younkers go off sometimes by the score. I've seen 'em trundled

out in fever and plague, egad, lying in rows, like plucked chickens in a poulterer's shop. And they say you've scarletina all about you, *here,* now; bad complaint, you know, that kills the little children. You need not frighten yourselves, though, because it must happen, sooner or later—die you must. It's the penalty, you know, because Eve once ate an apple.

Despite an occasionally vivid monologue like this, the plot is unfortunately stock, as Dingwell turns out to be not the villain he had appeared and Larkin is overthrown once again. LeFanu at this time seems searching for a theme, for something to replace the vein which had run dry. After a brief venture with romance he once again returns to the problem of evil and the human soul, but he can only describe the workings of wickedness, not explain them. Thus this novel and *A Lost Name* (1867–68), which followed it, are little more than suspense or murder mysteries. This last, a reworking of the short story "Some Account of the Latter Days of the Hon. Richard Marston of Dunoran," which in turn was redone as "The Evil Guest," has its share of shadowy intrigues and bloodletting, but it can offer only this surface. The psychological perception which had given life to his earlier works is at this time not so evident, and it is for this reason that the novels are something less than memorable.

It is with *Haunted Lives* (1868) that LeFanu returned to something of his old form in this tale of Laura Challys Gray and Alfred Dacre, alias Guy de Beaumirail. On the surface the plot concerns the attempt of Larkin and two of his associates, Levi and Gillespie, to fleece Laura of her fortune with the aid of de Beaumiral, whom Laura has doomed to debtors' prison. Because his lawsuits had contributed to her father's death and his jilting had broken her sister's heart, Laura had refused to allow Guy out of prison, but, with Larkin's aid, he comes to her for revenge in the person of Dacre. As a canny reader might have suspected, the two fall in love, and Dacre returns to prison rather than have Laura injured. Larkin is once again foiled, and it is only after Guy's death that Laura learns of the miscarrying of the affair.

The mood of the novel is sounded in the opening paragraph:

> The Old Brompton of my earlier recollections, with its silent lanes, its grass-plots, and flower knots, its towering trees, and those sober old houses of dusky red brick faced with white stone, which, set round with tall flower-pots and flowering shrubs and roses, had a character of old-world comfort, and even grace, has faded and broken up like a sunset city of cloud.

Essentially the subject of the novel is not the working of evil or the folly of retribution, but rather it is the shifting and treacherous nature of the world in which we live. One can never know the true status of one's own affairs, since all is shrouded in shadow and disguise, and happiness disappears before it ever can be savored. The romance of Laura and Guy is charged with passion and emotion, but neither ever allows the other a total view of an inner self. Nelson Browne has commented on "the atmosphere of frustrated passion that disturbs the reader with a faint sense of embarrassment,"[9] but

---

9. *Sheridan LeFanu*, p. 60.

it is pity at the futility of all this, rather than embarrassment, which LeFanu is attempting to evoke. At the heart of human affairs lie tragedy and failure, and Laura evidences her ultimate acceptance of all this in her later marriage to the bland Charles Mannering. What does it all matter, she seems to say, if one can never attain to real love and happiness?

Browne suspects that the affair of Laura and Guy is actually a picture of a Lesbian involvement, and he cites the descriptions of Guy as something less than manly:

> This face was very feminine. There was colour in the cheeks, and a soft lustre in those large eyes, with their long lashes, and a soft carmine touched the lips. The waving hair lay low upon a very white forehead. Altogether, the tints and formation of the face were feminine and delicate, and there was something of fire and animation, too.

Rather than dealing specifically with perverse sexuality, though, LeFanu is demonstrating the quality inherent in any sensitive and intelligent character. Guy appears effeminate, but there is no effeminacy in his actions and mingled thoughts of love and revenge. In the above description, "feminine and delicate" are balanced by "fire and animation," and it is this very duality which is the key to destruction. One can never resolve the conflicts of oppositions within one's soul, and this is why all individuals must remain unfulfilled. The outlook is certainly bleak, but for LeFanu it is at least a reasoned one. Chaos can be explained and understood, even if it cannot be overcome.

The Wyvern Mystery (1869) is a momentary lapse in the control LeFanu achieved over his materials, mainly because the focus of the plot jumps inconsistently. The first half of the novel deals with Alice Maybell and her tribulations with her weak husband, Charles Fairfield, while the second half encompasses a jump of eleven years and the theme of the lost heir. Alice's son Henry, familiarly known as "Fairy," had been spirited away from her after the death of Charles, but he is eventually returned through a circuitous route of happy coincidence and circumstance. The only scene with consistent power is one in which Alice is pursued by the murderous blind woman, Bertha Velderkaust:

> The whole thing was like a dream. The room seemed all a cloud. She could see nothing but the white figure that was still close, climbing swiftly over the bed, with one hand extended now and the knife in the other.

LeFanu's three final novels continue the theme of *Haunted Lives*. The first, *Checkmate* (1871), is interestingly enough something of a reworking of *The Cock and Anchor*. Walter Longcluse, like de Beaumiral, seeks to revenge himself on Alice Arden here for her spurning of his proposal of marriage. Gaining control over her brother Richard through his gambling debts, as did Nicholas Blarden in a similar situation, he intends to force a marriage and to destroy her family's name:

> Mere cruelty gives me no pleasure: well for some people it don't. Revenge does make me happy: well for some people if it didn't. Except for those I love or those I hate, I live for none. The rest live for me. I owe them no more

than I do this rotten stick. Let them rot and fatten my
land; let them burn and bake my bread.

The stumbling block to Longcluse's plan, however, lies
within himself, for he cannot erase all traces of his love
for Alice. He has changed his name from Yelland Mace
to Longcluse and changed his face with the aid of the
plastic surgeon Vanboeren to cover up a murder he had
committed years earlier, but he still cannot resolve his
feelings and intentions. Once again the theme of disguise and making over appears, and once again this
proves no solution for the inner man. Confronted with
his crimes, Longcluse cannot carry out his revenge, returns the note which Richard had forged, and commits
suicide. Like Maud Vernon in *The Rose and the Key*
(1871), who is imprisoned in an insane asylum, he can
make no sense out of the absurd universe which is re-
volving around him. It is an impossible world which
LeFanu is presenting, in which there is neither order
nor harmony, where characters move blindly and aim-
lessly like the ignorant armies on Matthew Arnold's
darkling plain. One might wonder if the struggles in
the novels here somehow foreshadow the futile striving
of some of Irishman Samuel Beckett's characters, as poor
Watt seeks to solve the mystery of the establishment of
Mr. Knott.

Willing to Die (1873), published shortly before his
death, may be seen as LeFanu's final and most comprehensive statement of the meaninglessness he had come
to see in existence. Ethel Ware begins by issuing a dis-
claimer against all artistry and says that she will set
down everything just as it was: "I shall write it down

with as much confidence as if I had actually seen it; in that respect imitating, I believe, all great historians, modern and ancient." It has been complained that this novel offers little action and is devoid of characteristic moments of terror, but LeFanu has other aims here. We are to watch Ethel become exposed to life, to follow her gradual maturation. She is to become involved with the strange Marston, the love of her life, to combat poverty alone on the streets of London, and finally to be rewarded for her determination with great wealth, though she is to lose her ill-fated lover. She has awakened to life and proved her inner worth through her triumph over the forces of adversity, yet she is left embittered, rather than equable, and is indeed willing to die. The Protestant myth seems somehow empty, and Ethel has much in common with Rachel and Dorcas in *Wylder's Hand.*

With the objectivity of the above-mentioned historian, LeFanu has chronicled the life of an intelligent and sensitive girl who keenly strives to perceive a meaning behind what happens to her. Ultimately, however, she is forced to realize that there is none, that all that awaits in the future is death. She can do nothing but retire into solitude to await her fate, a fate which stares at her from the faces of the old:

> Their memories are busy with a phantom world that passed away before we were born. They are puckered masks and glassy eyes, peeping from behind the door of the sepulchre that stands ajar, closing little by little to shut them in forever. . . . The world is for the young— it belongs to them, and time makes us ugly, and despised, and solitary, and prepares for our unrequited removal,

for nature has ordained that death shall trouble the
pleasure and economy of the vigorous, high-spirited world
as little as may be.

The sombre moroseness which builds throughout these
pages is all the more horrible in its rationality, and here
is certainly the greatest terror which LeFanu created.
There can be no escape from the bleakness which per-
vades the very fiber of society, so that one action must
be just as empty as any other. There are no ghosts or
phantoms here, since they can contribute no further
depth to the horror of realizing that all has been and
will be for nothing. Faced with a complete and utter
realization of this, there can have been little more that
Sheridan LeFanu could have wished to write. In the
progression of his novels we can trace a steady movement from a healthy optimism and belief that man can
prevail to a final position of fatalistic nihilism. As he
retreated in his own seclusion more and more into himself, he could find nothing to justify the workings of a
world which seemed to act upon no fixed principle at
all. And actually who is to say, in these times, that he
was completely off the mark?

One would not want to overestimate the talents of
Sheridan LeFanu as a novelist, yet it does seem clear
that his critical reputation is in need of an upgrading.
Contained within his works is a great wealth of psychological insight, which is his special forte. At his best he
is a social commentator and an explorer of the individual, fusing both pursuits into a unified whole. As

V. S. Pritchett puts it, "he has, within his limits, an individual accent and a flawless virtuosity."[10] To classify him simply as a creator of suspense and mystery is to do him a gross injustice and to miss the central thematic threads with which he weaves. Viewing him from this perspective, it is really not so hard to see why James Joyce would adopt him as one of his models for his own examinations of personality.

Like Joyce, too, LeFanu possesses an extraordinary sympathy for and understanding of the feminine mind. In Rachel Lake, Maud Ruthyn, Laura Gray, and Ethel Ware he offers living, breathing characters, and a reader's interest is held as much by their presentations as it is by the toils which involve them. Women, to LeFanu, are essentially tragic figures, since they are able to perceive the inequities which exist in their own situations and in the society around them, yet they are powerless to effect any significant change. They possess a quality of introspection which is lacking in his men, and thus they seem closer to a true evaluation of existence. Faced with an insoluble situation, they can only turn their backs on the world in which they cannot live to escape the round of meaningless actions which society requires. While LeFanu's men are often tortured, Byronic people who welter in their own passions (Henry Ashwoode, Guy de Beaumirail, Richard Marston), his women attempt to understand themselves and in so doing are usually spiritually destroyed. It is this sensitivity and perception which separates them from the usual run of Victorian heroines and makes of them characters who

---

10. *The Living Novel and Later Appreciations*, p. 122.

seem more at home in the twentieth than in the nineteenth century.

Nelson Browne feels that LeFanu's rendering of strong emotion is rather lacklustre and that the actual passion of human relationships is usually missing in the novels:

> Affection, gentle, filial, and dutiful, he portrays in all its delicacy, nobility, and pathos, but the comforting glow of this genial fire has none of the ardour of passion. No doubt in contenting himself with the demure and almost Platonic love-making that we find in his stories he subscribed to a middle-class convention which he shrank from setting at defiance.[11]

Whether or not middle-class convention is involved here, the fact remains that any truly *graphic* presentation of sexuality would have been uncharacteristic of his time. In actuality, however, there is a great deal of passion and sexuality in the novels, not all of it hiding beneath the surface. In *Guy Deverell,* for example, the affair of Jekyl and Lady Jane is presented quite openly, and it is Jane's passion and despair at the destruction of their liaison which finally cause her death. Dorcas Brandon's desire for Stanley Lake, too, is as much physical as it is intellectual. Many of the female relationships presented are close and intense, as in *Wylder's Hand* and *Willing to Die,* and *Haunted Lives* is overtly sensual in its highly romantic presentation of love. The whole question of the female relationships has led some critics to point to a suspicion of Lesbianism (most strongly evident in the short story "Carmilla," discussed

11. *Sheridan LeFanu,* p. 123.

earlier), and it does seem that this should at once be admitted. There is always a heavy aura of sensuality about these dark and brooding women characters which hints at something more than purely friendly entanglements. Whether or not LeFanu was wrestling with some kind of suppressed homosexuality within himself remains, of course, something we can never know, and ungrounded suppositions would serve no purpose. The point is that LeFanu's work, rather than conveying the insipid sentimentality of a Little Nell, contains much more the highly charged sexuality of *Wuthering Heights.* If one is to draw a whole character, then the sexual must certainly be included. LeFanu does the best he can within the limits which have been set up for him.

At the same time, one must admit that LeFanu's practice of often extending a short story into a novel can occasionally be a treacherous one. In *Uncle Silas* and *Checkmate* the process works well, but *The Wyvern Mystery* becomes a disaster. The extension of the narrative is instrumental in building the tension of *Uncle Silas* and the reworking of theme in *Checkmate* illuminates the change which had come about in LeFanu's apprehension of his environment, but the added length in *Wyvern* merely makes the story unmanageable. It should be granted, too, that LeFanu sometimes has trouble maintaining interest over a long narrative, but he is successful more times than not. His basic technique is to reveal character and situation through a gradual process of accrual, to let mood and atmosphere become his spokesmen. At his worst he can lapse into moral didacticism, but at his best he allows the works themselves to imply their meanings. In many instances he will set up a highly defined mood of impending danger or catastrophe through his description of the natural scene or of the old mansions of which he seems so fond. It is when he lets such descriptions as these do his work for him that he is most successful.

Most notable throughout the works of LeFanu is the sense one usually gets of control, the feeling that there is an artistic purpose to what we are viewing which we will realize if we think about it. Almost none of the novels is overly garrulous, and few contain a panorama of subplots which are not somehow or other related to the central theme. It would seem that LeFanu considered himself more an artist than a simple storyteller like Carleton or Lover. The novels are meant to be representative of a body of thought and are the production of a *weltanschauung* rather than an impression. As LeFanu himself said in *Uncle Silas*: "This world is a parable—the habitation of symbols—the phantoms of spiritual things immortal shown in material shape," and he is concerned with the explication of these symbols. The "fiery shorthand" of which Yeats spoke is, in this case, the attempt of Sheridan LeFanu to decipher the life he saw around him and to transmit it in some kind of understandable form through the medium of the novel.

In his study of the nineteenth-century Irish novel, Thomas Flanagan defines the basic difference between the English and Irish works of art as follows:

> The English novelist was concerned with social choice and personal morality, which are the great issues of European fiction. But to the Irish novelist these were subordi-

nated to questions of race, creed, and nationality—
questions which tend of their nature to limit the range
and power of fiction.[12]

Later, he will state that both Maturin and LeFanu are
definitely outside the tradition of conventional Irish
literature: "it is significant, perhaps, that both of these
highly gifted members of the Ascendancy should have
turned to tales whose somber and uncanny atmosphere
seeks to transcend the immediacies of social fact."[13]
While Maturin may be guilty on the second count, one
might wonder if the condemnation of LeFanu takes
the totality of his writings into consideration. In neither
case are these statements apt descriptions of LeFanu
as a novelist, for it is just such concerns as these which
are at the center of his work. Beneath the particular
the universal is always the object in question.

Though the point has been made that LeFanu in
many of his novels is documenting the predicament of
the Protestant Ascendancy (as in *The Cock and Anchor,
Torlogh O'Brien,* and *Uncle Silas*), later novels such
as *Haunted Lives, Checkmate,* and *Willing to Die* are
primarily involved with personal morality and individual choice, and these topics are evident in some degree
in the earliest of his works. More and more he comes to
feel that solutions, if they can be arrived at in any way,
can be propounded only for the individual. No viable
social blueprint can be sketched out until the citizens
within the society have defined their own personal prop-

12. *The Irish Novelists: 1800–1850* (New York: Columbia University
Press, 1959), p. 35.
13. *Ibid.,* p. 46.

ositions. Kinship must first be moral before it can be racial or national.

Thus LeFanu does not touch at all upon the religious question, and never seems to acknowledge any antagonism between Protestant and Catholic. (The only exception to this is *Willing to Die,* where the Jesuit Order is portrayed as the league of fiends which infests *Melmoth the Wanderer.*) Far from ignoring the religious issue, however, LeFanu's feeling is that this, along with the problem of Home Rule, is a question which at present simply cannot be resolved to anyone's satisfaction. He is not transcending—he is moving behind the immediate problem to what lies at its roots. Charles Archer or Jekyl Marlowe may be Protestant, Catholic, or Jewish; it makes little difference. It is not the formal religious affiliation or the political party of the Irishman which is of greatest importance. Essentially, the individual in a crumbling social situation is not even capable of choosing right over wrong or tolerance over bigotry. Here are the choices which first must be made, and here are the problems with which the novelist comes to grips.

Rather than transporting us out of the present, as might a tale of science fiction, the somber and uncanny atmospheres which LeFanu creates are totally representative of the here and now. What could be more somber, and yet more realistic, than the ultimate plight of Ethel Ware? What could be more illustrative of the gap in understanding between the generations than the cross-purposes of Varbarriere and Guy Deverell? The dark and depressive physical surroundings of the characters are symbolic of their internal, mental states. Instead of limiting his artistic vision, it would seem that the seclusion of Sheridan LeFanu was a blessing in disguise, for it preserved him from the pitfalls of immersion in immediate social concern. Yet at the same time it induced him to concentrate upon the larger issues which were the true shapers of his time.

It is significant, too, that LeFanu produced no narrative of education or *bildungsroman,* no character to parallel Pip or David Copperfield. While Dickens will follow such young men as these, who are tested by experience and who end with a pretty firm grasp upon the goals of their lives and the means they must and should utilize to achieve them, LeFanu's people are usually left all in the dark: not darkness in the sense that they have necessarily succumbed to evil, but darkness in the sense that they remain unable to see their way through existence. The education of the protagonists of LeFanu would seem to go on indefinitely, never attaining to a surety of meaning or purpose. This is not to denigrate the Englishman, but only to point out that Dickens's faith in England as it stands is not paralleled by LeFanu's belief in Ireland. With LeFanu the search is never-ending, and there exists no authority to which the individual can turn. Unlike John Banim, Gerald Griffin, and William Carleton, who are mainly concerned with the specific Irishman, LeFanu deals with men in an Irish situation. As he phrases it in the verse drama "Beatrice," published in 1865:

> Man upon his journey hies—
> A chequered course and variable,

Walking through life as he is shown
By gleams through yawning darkness thrown—
By lights that fall from Paradise
And hues that cross from hell.

Can we read his words or ways?
Whence he acts, or whereto thinks?
A vapour changing as we gaze,
An utterance of the Sphinx.
Still the man our judgement baulks;
Good is he? or, is he evil?
At his right an Angel walks,
At his left a Devil.

One final question which remains to be asked, then, is whether Sheridan LeFanu is to be considered an "Irish" writer whose works contribute to a steadily progressing tradition of Irish literature. Does he bear resemblances and correspondences to what is generally described as a national literature? Douglas Hyde, of course, in his *Literary History of Ireland,* answers the question in the negative, since he considers that only works which are written in Gaelic can truly be called Irish, but for LeFanu we will have to adjust the definition a bit. As an Anglo-Irishman he is just as attuned to his nation as any of his countrymen, and in fact his novels help to lead Irish literature out of the Lover-Lever syndrome. They do attempt to place the protagonist in a more universal context. In his own time, LeFanu was extremely popular and very influential in his role as editor of the *Dublin University Magazine* (the journal at that time had no connection with the college), and his attention to more general and ethical problems may certainly be seen as something of a link to the work of George Moore and James Joyce. Though LeFanu produced nothing so outwardly Irish as *Esther Waters* or *Dubliners,* he does show his contemporaries that literature emanating from Dublin need not carry with it a collection of stage Irishmen or peasant folklore.

He demonstrates that Ireland need not be only John Bull's other island, and that if Irish literature is to grow it must break the bonds of shortsightedness and internal inspection. "Relevance" is a many-headed monster, and "relevance to what" is something not so easily answered. As the nineteenth century matured, Irishmen began to see themselves as citizens of Europe rather than of the British Empire, and the political contributions of such as Charles Stewart Parnell and Padraic Pearse needed to be supplemented by the more spiritual examinations of Irish artists. Without exaggerating his role too much, one can say that Sheridan LeFanu played a part in the development and spread of this growing awareness.

Thus it appears that the novelist projects two radically different faces to his audience. As the public man and the artist he maintains an objective grasp upon the elements of his fiction, sifting the evidence at hand to find out where his society went wrong and what can be done about it. He is a champion of the honorable and the just, a believer in the ultimate value of the authentic and sincere human relationship, yet he can never reconcile his beliefs with a contemporary situation which seems to have forgotten or repudiated all that he holds dear. To himself, his values are not old fashioned, yet he never becomes strident or shrill in his attempt to halt the process of society's degeneration. Despite an ever-increasing disillusionment, he tests in work after work the aptness of his premises, searching for the avenue of behavior which can lead to fulfillment.

At the same time, as an individual human being who must live out the sterility and defeat of which he writes, LeFanu cannot help becoming one of his own protagonists. A tortured man like Richard Arden, or Guy de Beaumirail, or even Silas Ruthyn, he seems to utilize his art as a stabilizing force upon his own personal life. For him, the novels and their creation function as both purgation and catharsis, allowing him both the objectivity and involvement without which he cannot live. It is unfortunate that almost all of his personal papers have been either lost or destroyed, for the light they may have shed on his inner feelings might have helped us to understand him more deeply. Significantly, LeFanu continued writing up until his death, as if he could not bring himself to renounce completely the possibility of reaching an answer. S. M. Ellis recounts that LeFanu did most of his writing in his later years in the early hours of the morning, when he would awaken from a nightmare and "write for a couple of hours in that eerie period of the night when human vitality is at its lowest ebb and the Powers of Darkness rampant and terrifying."[14] It is a tribute to the strength of his inherent beliefs that he was able to hold out so long against futility and despair.

Though Sheridan LeFanu is generally regarded today as something of a second-rate novelist, it might be helpful to remember that none of the nineteenth-century

---

14. *Wilkie Collins, LeFanu, and Others*, p. 175.

Irish writers can be said to stand with George Eliot, Charles Dickens, or Thomas Hardy. Indeed, Irish literature was embryonic, just beginning to emerge into its own, but it laid the groundwork for the great masters of the succeeding century. Though it would be a bit exuberant to call for a revival of LeFanu, several of his novels certainly merit a reprinting, as literary testaments and as works of art in their own right. There is something about him which is appealing to a modern taste. If his witches are now mainly the province of the ghost-story devotee (he is honored by Montague Summers and M. R. James), nevertheless in the work of LeFanu inheres the spirit of the Ireland of his time, and for this alone it should be valuable to us today. His concern with his place in his contemporary society is basically that with which we are wrestling today.

Dreams played an important part in LeFanu's writings, and it is said that at the end of his life he was plagued with recurring nightmares which he could not escape. By this time he had become a total recluse, refusing to see even his closest old friends when they occasionally came to call. One such nocturnal phantasm involved an ancient and crumbling mansion on the point of toppling over while the dreamer was incapable of moving from the spot. On his death from a heart attack in February, 1873, his doctor is supposed to have commented that the house had claimed its victim at last. The career of Joseph Sheridan LeFanu was long and varied, and, despite his personal problems, he made a significant contribution to Irish literature. As his admirer and bibliographer S. M. Ellis describes his work: "in [it] . . . there is something akin to the panoramic pilgrimage of human life, the sunshine and the shadows, the joy and the tragedy, the happy song and the dirge of sorrow, the high lights of the hills of romance and the dark valley through which all must shudderingly pass ere they reach the oblivion of the tomb."[15]

15. *Wilkie Collins, LeFanu, and Others*, p. 179.

Selected Bibliography

THE PRINCIPAL WORKS OF JOSEPH SHERIDAN LEFANU

(Dates are first book-length publication)
1. *The Cock and Anchor.* Dublin and London: William Curry, 1845.
2. *The Fortunes of Colonel Torlogh O'Brien.* Dublin and London: William S. Orr, 1847.
3. *Ghost Stories and Tales of Mystery.* Dublin and London: William S. Orr, 1851.
4. *The House by the Churchyard.* London: Tinsley Bros., 1863.
5. *Wylder's Hand.* London: Richard Bentley, 1864.
6. *Uncle Silas.* London: Richard Bentley, 1864.
7. *Guy Deverell.* London: Richard Bentley, 1865.
8. *All in the Dark.* London: Richard Bentley, 1866.
9. *The Tenants of Malory.* London: Tinsley Bros., 1867.
10. *A Lost Name.* London: Richard Bentley, 1868.
11. *Haunted Lives.* London: Tinsley Bros., 1868.
12. *The Wyvern Mystery.* London: Tinsley Bros., 1869.
13. *Checkmate.* London: Hurst and Blackett, 1871.
14. *The Rose and the Key.* London: Chapman and Hall, 1871.
15. *Chronicles of Golden Friars.* London: Richard Bentley, 1871.
16. *In a Glass Darkly.* London: Richard Bentley, 1872.

17. *Willing to Die*. London: Hurst and Blackett, 1873.
18. *The Purcell Papers,* with a Memoir by A. P. Graves. London: Richard Bentley, 1880.
19. *The Poems of Joseph Sheridan LeFanu,* ed. A. P. Graves. London: Downey and Co., 1896.

Note: The most complete bibliography of the works is included at the end of his chapter on LeFanu in S. M. Ellis's *Wilkie Collins, LeFanu, and Others* (London: Constable, 1951) .

No full-length biography of LeFanu has been written.

CRITICAL STUDIES

Benson, E. F. "Sheridan LeFanu." *Spectator* (February, 1931) .

Bleiler, E. F. "Introduction," *Best Ghost Stories of J. S. LeFanu.* New York: Dover Publications, Inc., 1964.

Bowen, Elizabeth. "Introduction," *The House by the Churchyard.* New York: Stein & Day, 1968.

————. "Introduction," *Uncle Silas.* London: Cresset Press, Ltd., 1947.

Browne, Nelson. *Sheridan LeFanu.* London: Artur Barker, Ltd., 1951.

Ellis, S. M. *Wilkie Collins, LeFanu, and Others.* London: Constable, 1951.

Graves, A. P. *Irish Literary and Musical Studies.* London: Elkin Mathews, 1913.

————. *To Return to All That.* London: Jonathan Cape, 1930.

Kenton, Edna. "A Forgotten Creator of Ghosts: J. S. LeFanu, Possible Inspirer of the Brontes." *Bookman* (1929) .

LeFanu, W. R. *Seventy Years of Irish Life.* New York: Macmillan, 1893.

Lougheed, W. C. "An Addition to the LeFanu Bibliography." *N&Q* (1964) .

Lovecraft, H. P. *Supernatural Horror in Literature*. New York: Ben Abramson, 1945.

Penzoldt, Peter. *The Supernatural in Fiction*. New York: Humanities Press, 1965.

Pritchett, V. S. "Introduction," *In A Glass Darkly*. London: John Lehmann, 1947.

————. *The Living Novel and Later Appreciations*. New York: Random House, 1964.

Sayers, Dorothy, ed. *An Omnibus of Crime*. New York: Garden City Publishing Co., 1929.

Scott, Kenneth. "LeFanu's 'The Room in the Dragon Volant.' " *LHR* 10 (1968) : 25–32.

Shroyer, Frederick. "Introduction," *Uncle Silas*. New York: Dover Publications, Inc., 1966.

Summers, Montague. "J. S. LeFanu and His Houses." *Architectural Design and Construction* (May, 1932) .